I Am Home

UNLOCKING THE GIFTS OF SELF-DISCOVERY AND MEDIUMSHIP

By Julie Dart

DEDICATION

I want to thank my mother for being supportive of my gift. When I was younger, she validated the feelings and premonitions that I had, which is what I needed at the time. "Thank you, Mom. I am eternally grateful."

CONTENTS

ACKNOWLEDGMENTS

Thank you to all of my college friends for helping me view my gift as a positive, rather than a negative, gift.

To my friend Tammy, I appreciate all of the literature you gave me and for encouraging me to acknowledge my gift as a medium. It means a lot to me, as does your friendship.

To Barbie, I am grateful for your message encouraging me to write this book. I consider that a pivotal moment in deciding to share my story.

Heidi, thank you for cheering me on and giving me the confidence to keep moving in this direction. I have felt your love and support from the very beginning.

Thank you to my children. I know at times, my gift seemed strange or difficult to understand. As we grew together, you both reminded me of how much my gift was helping other people, which was the touchstone that I used to keep going. I love you both and I am so lucky to have you in my life.

Lastly, I would like to thank my clients and friends for letting me share their experiences. I believe these stories will help others realize that their loved ones, who have passed away, are around them, providing loving support from the other side[+].

[+]I am not a doctor or a psychologist. If you are dealing with a physical illness or having psychological issues, please consult a licensed doctor or psychologist.

CHAPTER 1
MY STORY

When I was younger, I wasn't aware that I had the gift of being a medium. All I remember was that I sporadically "knew" things. I didn't understand how or why I knew these things, and I surely didn't think it was because I had a gift.

I never heard the term "medium" when I was little so I didn't even know what it was. It's not like we had mediums come to school on career day and tell us what they did. I wish that were the case. I would have been able to learn who I was and therefore embrace my gift when I was younger. Instead, I grew up feeling like I was weird, too sensitive, and that there was something wrong with me.

It wasn't until I met my friend Tammy, at the age of 30, that I heard the term "medium." Within the first couple of months of hanging out with Tammy, she could see that I had an ability to "know" things. She told me many times that she thought I was a psychic medium. I assured her that my "knowing" was just common sense, but Tammy was convinced that I had a gift. She gave me a variety of books on the subject of mediumship. Most of the information in the books resonated with me so I continued to read them.

Reading those books led me to acknowledge and activate my own gift. I refer to this as my spiritual awakening, though at the time it felt more like a midlife crisis. I was 36 years old, married, had two beautiful children, and was working as a recruiter. But my marriage was ending, my health was fading, and I was tired all the time. I felt like something was missing, but I had no idea what it was.

That is, until I embraced my gift. Then it was like my entire life made sense. My health improved and I had more joy in my life.

While learning to open up to my gift, I wanted to make sure the energy I was receiving was from light and love. I chose to call upon God and the Angels to help me do my work. To me, God and the Angels are loving energy that remain by our side, helping to guide us. I feel no judgement while working with this energy, only love and acceptance. This process works best for me while opening up communication to the other side. For this reason, I refer to my medium sessions as Angel Readings.

Now, instead of wishing that I wasn't so sensitive, I have embraced my gift. I've had the privilege of seeing how much an Angel Reading can help comfort people in their time of grief.

My hope is that after reading this book, you will feel uplifted and know that there is always loving energy around you. And that by knowing this, you will understand that you are never alone.

CHAPTER 2
EXPERIENCES

When I was about five years old I remember my grandmother, who lived across town, coming to visit me. I told my mother that Grandmother was in my room and she was trying to tell me something, but I didn't understand what she was saying.

"No, Julie," my mom said. "Honey, she's not here, you must have been dreaming."

The next day, we received a phone call that my grandmother had passed away. My mother assured me that my vision of Grandma was real. "She probably came to visit you before she went to heaven," she said.

In the fifth grade, I remember telling my classmates that we were going to have a substitute teacher because our teacher was sick, and the substitute was going to be a bald man. When a bald man appeared to teach our class that day, I realized from the students' reaction how strange it was that I knew this information. That day I made a promise to myself that I would never open up to people like that again. I stopped sharing those kinds of things and became withdrawn.

When I was in college, before cell phones and Facebook, everything opened up again. I would just know things, like where my friends were, and I was able to track them down so we could make plans for the day. My friends often joked with me saying things like, "Julie will know where we can find so-and-so because she's psychic." I assured my friends it wasn't a psychic ability it was just common sense.

It was difficult for me to have close friends or boyfriends who weren't honest with me because somehow, I knew when they were being dishonest.

One time I went home to visit my parents and while I was there I had a horrible dream that my boyfriend had cheated on me. In the dream, I saw there was a BBQ, and I could see the people who were there. When I woke from the dream I was physically sick. I phoned the friends who were at the BBQ in my dream and told them what I had seen. They both denied it, but I knew I was right and proceeded to pressure them until they told me the truth. My friends couldn't believe that I knew exactly what had happened.

It wasn't until the age of twenty-five that I started to realize that the dreams I was having weren't just dreams, they were more like premonitions. And the times where I "knew things," had to be something more than just common sense.

I had just graduated from college and moved to the Bay Area. One morning, at about 3:30 a.m., I had a dream that my college friend Bobby was crying and rocking back and forth in a fetal position. I was so upset by the dream that I couldn't go back to sleep. I tried to ignore the feelings I was having, but I couldn't. I felt that I should call Bobby to make sure he was okay. I hadn't spoken to him in over a year and didn't even know if he still lived in our college town. I called information, and they were able to connect me to his number.

I explained to Bobby how, in my dream, he had been crying. I shared with him how I was sure it was just a stupid dream, and once he told me that he was okay, I would let him go.

"Julie," he said, "I just received a phone call last night, letting me know that my mom died. I was just getting ready to head home when the phone rang and it's you calling to tell me about a dream you had about me. This is kind of freaking me out and I have to go, goodbye."

I hung up the phone and began to cry. I cried for Bobby and his pain, and I cried because I was scared. I didn't know what was happening to me. Why was I having dreams that were about real life situations? And what did this mean? I had no idea where to go to receive answers for these questions.

I met Tammy five years later when I was 30. It seemed like from the moment I met her she began telling me that I was psychic. When we went out together, she would tell people that I could tell them their future, and we would both laugh. But one time she mentioned this to a family sitting next to us in a hotel lobby. The family members came one by one to receive a message from me and thanked me after we were done. Tammy joked with me that she was going to be my assistant and handle all of my appointments.

About five months later, I had another dream that I shared with Tammy. In this dream, my ex-boyfriend, Mike, was getting married at the mission in our college town. When I told Tammy about the dream, she encouraged me to call him, so I did. Just like with Bobby, I had lost touch with

Mike, and had no idea where he was living or if he was dating anyone. Then, I remembered where he worked while we were dating so I tried that number and sure enough, he still worked there. I told Mike about the dream I had and he started laughing and confirmed everything; he was, indeed, getting married at the mission.

"Do me a favor," he said, "if you ever have a dream that I am going to be in a car crash, please call me."

This is when Tammy started to give me books about mediums and psychics.

CHAPTER 3
THE AWAKENING

One of the books my friend Tammy gave me was *Sacred Contracts* by Caroline Myss. Because I found it difficult to read, I put it aside after the first two chapters. I feel the need to mention this book because soon after reading it, I had a strange dream. This dream pointed me in the direction I needed to go to open up to my gift.

In my dream, there was a woman looking

at books in a bookstore with me. The woman gently touched my hand and said, "Julie, you need to find your Angels." Then, a fire engine raced by us, inside the store. When I awoke from this dream, my heart was beating incredibly fast and I was sweating profusely. I immediately wrote down my dream and what I thought it meant. *Julie this is a 911 call; find your Angels.*

When I shared this dream with my mother, she mentioned that there was a woman named Karen who did readings at her friend's café. My mother took me to meet her. The woman gave me what she called an Angel Reading. The woman asked God and the Angels, in a prayer, to help her to receive any information that would be healing for me. The reading was very clear, and I felt very safe and at peace after it was complete. This woman truly had a gift.

About a month after my Angel Reading with Karen something interesting happened. I was on a vacation in Hawaii with my husband and two kids, and I was reading a book about Angels. In the book it mentioned how you could call upon your Angels for help, and it explained how to do it. My husband had taken the kids to the pool, so I decided to try calling upon the Angels for help: "Dear God and Angels, please tell me what you need me to know."

And I heard a loud voice say, "Julie, you can't have wine; it is poisoning your body, and you are lacking enzymes. Your body is depleted, which is why you are so tired. And the supplements you are taking as vitamins are toxic."

This was not a disembodied voice, but rather a voice inside my head. It was kind of like my voice when I'm thinking, but different. The voice was telling me about enzymes and how my vitamins were toxic. These were things I didn't even know about. It was a strange sensation because I was nervous, but yet calm at the same time.

I asked, "Why are you coming to me as a voice inside my head, and how do I know that you are my Angels?"

The voice said, "As long as the voice tells you to do good things, it is from your Angels, but if you ever hear a voice telling you to do harm to yourself or someone else, run and get help."

At this point, I was scared and wanted confirmation that I was okay. I had no idea who to turn to, but then I remembered Karen, the woman who gave me the Angel

Reading the month before. I grabbed my phone to call Karen, but when I picked it up, she was calling me.

"Hello, Julie?" she said with deep concern, "are you okay?"

"I think so," I said. "Why are you calling me?"

"I was in a meeting and I kept hearing, 'Call Julie, call Julie!' so I excused myself from my meeting and called you."

"Oh, I'm reading this book about Angels and it tells you how to say a prayer to God and your Angels so that you can receive guidance, so I did that. And I heard a loud voice, but it was strange because the voice was inside my head. I don't know if this is making sense," I told her.

Then Karen said, "As long as the voice is telling you to do good things, it is an Angel, but if you ever hear the voice tell you to do something bad to yourself or someone else, run and get help."

I was in shock as I heard Karen's words because they were the same words I had just written down.

"You are fine," Karen said, "The voice you are hearing is from your Angels. Feel free to call me if you need anything."

I continued to read more books about Angels. After the fourth book, I felt I needed to learn "hands-on healing," but I didn't know what it was called. Once again, I asked Karen and she told me that "hands-on healing" was called Reiki and that she could teach it to me. I began giving Reiki treatments to myself for a couple of months. I kept moving up levels with the Reiki and I quickly became a Reiki Master. While learning about Reiki, I continued to pray to God and the Angels. I also prayed to God and the Angels for help with anyone I was giving a Reiki treatment to.

One time, while giving a Reiki treatment to a woman, I heard a voice say, "Her dad has passed away. Tell her that her dad is very proud of her and says that she is a good mother and that he loves her very much."

"I don't want to tell her that," I argued with the voice. "I don't even know if her dad is dead or if she even has kids."

"Tell her this, she needs to know. It will help her heal," repeated the voice.

"I don't want to. What if I'm not right?"

The voice continued, "Ask her if her dad wore glasses and she will say 'yes.' Then, ask her if he read the paper every morning and she will say 'yes.' Then, tell her that her father came to you during the session

and that he is very proud of her and that
she is a great mother and that he loves
her."

After the Reiki session, I asked her the
questions my Angels proposed. She
confirmed that her dad wore glasses and
read the newspaper every day. Then I
shared with her that her father had come
to me during the Reiki session and told
me to tell her that he was proud of her,
that she was a great mother, and that he
loves her. She wept and thanked me. It was
the anniversary of her father's passing. She
was the youngest child and they were very
close. She shared that she missed him very

much.

"Thank you," she said. "Now I know that he is with me."

"It will be very healing for her," repeated the voice, as I was leaving.

I desperately wanted to learn how to give an Angel Reading, and assure I was doing it properly, because it now appeared that Angel messages were coming through in my Reiki sessions. Even though I was receiving confirmation that the messages I was giving to people were accurate, I doubted myself. I felt I needed to learn more about the process so I could be more confident in sharing the messages I was receiving.

One night, while reading about Angels, I noticed a website. It was late and my family was asleep. I grabbed my computer and visited the site. The site mentioned that there was a class on how to become a certified Angel Reader. The class would teach people how to perform an Angel Reading. This was exactly what I was looking for.

I saw that there was a class in Laguna, California, but the class was seven months away. The next class was in Hawaii. It would have been less expensive for me to wait and go to the class in Laguna, but I felt the need to go to this class as soon as I could. So, I pulled out my credit card and signed up for the class in Hawaii. This was not like me at all. I always asked my husband before signing up for these things and would never spend that kind of money on myself, but I knew I had to go.

When morning came I regretted being so impulsive.

"That was too much money," I told myself. "I will tell them I made a mistake and I need a refund."

But first, I had to get my kids ready for school. I went to my daughter's room and started to wake her up.

She slowly opened her eyes and said, "Mommy, are you going to go to Hawaii to learn about Angels so you can come back here and teach people about their Angels?"

I stood by her bed in shock. "What did you say, honey?"

"You should go to Hawaii and learn about Angels so you can come back and teach other people about their Angels. I think you're going to be very good at it," she said.

There was no way she could have known that I signed up for that class. I hadn't told anyone, and my husband and kids were all asleep when I was on the computer. I smiled and felt like Kevin Costner in the movie *Field of Dreams.*

"Julie," I said to myself, "you are going to Hawaii!"

CHAPTER 4
LESSONS

Becoming a practicing medium took some time. I trained for many years before I started my business. I had previously worked as a branch manager and a regional trainer at an employment company. I found success in those positions because I treated my customers and co-workers with courtesy and respect. It was important to me to do the same as I launched my own business.

Two important things I learned early on were that I needed to improve my eating habits and I needed to learn how to set healthy boundaries with my clients. I found my readings were clearer when I ate organic food and drank water with electrolytes. I had to completely stop drinking alcohol and was down to one caffeinated beverage per day. Setting healthy boundaries was needed—not because of my clients, they were wonderful, but it was something I needed to do for myself.

I not only wanted to help people, I

wanted to save them from their pain. I had to constantly remind myself that my clients had a loving source around them. It was up to my clients to decide if they wanted to connect to that loving source and what they wanted to call it. I could act only as a bridge and lovingly share the information I was receiving, while praying that they would find the healing they needed. Admittedly, I made mistakes along the way.

My biggest regret was seeing the highest potential of someone's journey and conveying it as a certainty. I refer to this as "wishful thinking" in readings. I now know that when I see the highest potential for my client's situation, I need to let them know that it is something that will require some work on their part.

I also had to learn how to communicate with the other side. It was different than talking to a person who was alive. I compare it to a game of charades. In each Angel Reading, I would take my client's hand and start with an intention, "God and Angels, what do I need to know about this person (I would add their name here)?" Soon after saying this, I would close my eyes and start to see, feel, and hear things that the spirits on the other side wanted me to share with their loved one.

When spirits from the other side come to me in my readings, they begin to show me pictures in my mind. I refer to this process as "coming forward." These pictures can be anything from a woman, to a butterfly, a rock band, a farm, an airplane, or even a gnome. They are basically hints of what would best describe them to the person I am giving the Angel Reading to. I had to learn to relay the pictures I saw, even if they didn't make sense to me. The pictures would usually make sense and mean a great deal to the person I was giving the

Angel Reading to.

If my client didn't understand what the pictures that I was describing meant, then I would start to feel something. This feeling would further confirm which spirit the message was from. Sometimes I would taste smoke in my mouth, indicating that the spirit on the other side was a smoker. Other times, I would be overwhelmed with feelings of love, similar to the feelings I have for my own son and daughter. This feeling would reveal that the spirit coming forward had to be their mother or father.

In other instances, I couldn't talk or move. When this occurred, I would know

that the person coming forward was in a
coma before they passed away. To my
frustration, spirits don't usually share with
me how they passed away. I often wish
they would, as it would give their loved
one further confirmation. However, I am
comforted in knowing that the spirits are
trying their hardest to give me messages
to help their loved one heal in the best
way that they can.

Some people have the illusion that a
medium can see everything and give you
all of the answers to your questions. This
is simply not true. We all have lessons;
God and the Angels can help get us

through them, but they can't help us skip a lesson, and neither can a medium. A medium can confirm that your loved ones are with you and help you see that you are loved and supported so you can have the courage to reach your full potential here on the earth's plane.

CHAPTER 5
READINGS

The following are examples of real life readings I have given to clients. Please note that some of the names have been altered to protect their privacy.

—Julie Dart

JEFF

Jeff came to me after he lost his mother. He said she was his best friend and he didn't know how he would keep going without her.

At the beginning of his reading, as with all of my readings, I set an intention, "God and Angels, please show me what I need to know about Jeff."

As I said this, I saw in my mind a lot of kids at what felt like his childhood home.

It looked like Jeff and his friends were on a baseball team. His mother was smiling and handing them snacks. I shared these images with Jeff.

"Yes," he said. "That's what I loved about my mom. She always had the team over after our games and fed us tons of food. My mom loved kids and kids loved her."

I heard the song "Butterfly Kisses" and shared it with Jeff. His eyes filled with tears.

"I can't believe you can hear that," he said. "My mom and I always gave each other butterfly kisses."

Jeff apologized for crying, so I reassured

him that it was good to cry, as it showed how much he loved his mother.

Jeff told his father, Tom, about his Angel Reading. About a month later, Tom flew out to have a reading with me. Although I offer readings by phone, Tom wanted to meet me in person. As Jeff and Tom entered my office, I could feel how nervous Tom was. When clients are nervous, I can feel their energy so I have to calm myself down and remember that these are their feelings, not mine. Once I do that, I am calm and better prepared for their reading.

I held Tom's hand and said, "God and Angels, please tell me what I need to know about Tom."

Shortly after, I saw images of a young woman walking down the stairs while family members and Tom waited at the bottom of the staircase. I then saw the woman trip. When I told Tom, he laughed and said she had tripped at the beginning of their courtship and he had caught her at the bottom of the steps. That was the moment he knew he was going to marry her one day.

"Good," I said. "I'm glad she's coming in so clearly."

I closed my eyes to see what else his wife would show me.

"She's playing the piano and talking about a teacher."

"Yes, she played the piano and she was a teacher," Tom confirmed.

Next, I saw her standing by a car, but instead of getting in through the door, she climbed in through the window. Tom confirmed that one of his first cars had a broken passenger door so she would have to enter through the driver's side or climb through the passenger window to get in. We all laughed, and then I closed my eyes again.

I told Tom that his wife seemed to be telling me that he wasn't taking care of himself, eating enough, or going to family gatherings. Tom said that was true. He hadn't felt like doing those things now that she was gone. I mentioned to Tom that his wife was showing me the movie *Up*, emphasizing the couple in the movie. Tom's son, Jeff, who was in the room with us, said that *Up* was the movie he had told him about a few days earlier. I told Jeff that this was his mom's way of showing me that she was aware of Jeff and Tom's conversation regarding the movie.

"Loved ones, who have passed away, will try to show us that they are still around us and aware of what's going on. You may not be able to see them anymore, but their spirit is still alive, and she watches over you," I said.

I told Tom that his wife understood how difficult it was for him to keep going, but she wanted him to do it for their kids and grandkids, and for her. She liked to live vicariously through Tom so when he hugged the grandkids and read stories to them, she was able to share in that experience as well. Tom promised he would try.

The reading was complete. After a few weeks, Tom told me he was happy to have received the reading. And though he still missed his wife physically being with him,

he now felt comfort and a sense of peace

in knowing that she was around him and

watching over him.

CAROL

Carol was a tough woman. I could tell she had her guard up and would really test me, making sure that I'd have the correct information. I said that I would start her reading and if she didn't feel the information was correct, then she didn't have to pay me.

"Okay," she said. This helped her relax a bit.

I asked for her hand and set my

intention: "God and Angels, please tell me what I need to know about Carol."

In my mind, I saw an older woman come forward and told Carol, "This feels like your grandmother."

"No, both of my grandmothers are still alive," she said, sitting with her arms crossed.

"Interesting," I said, "because she's making me feel like she helped raise you."

"No," Carol said abruptly.

"Can I ask you something? Were you raised by your parents?" I asked.

"No," she said, "I was adopted by my

great aunt."

"Oh," I said, "and has that great aunt passed away?"

"Yes," said Carol.

"Okay, sorry," I said. "That was me misreading who it was, but I knew it was an elderly woman who helped raise you."

I continued, "She is coming forward and making me feel like you would say thank God for her because she took you in when no one else wanted to."

Carol nodded.

I said, "She is saying 'you have it backwards;' *she* is thanking God for *you*.

She is saying that you were not a burden like you might have thought, you were a blessing. When you came into her life, her kids where older and had moved out, and her husband had passed away, and she was all alone. Then, you came along and she was so happy to have you in her life. You made her feel like she had a purpose and you made her feel young again. She loved being with you."

Trying to hold back tears, Carol began to cry. I told her what I told Jeff when he cried and added that it was healing to release tears.

I closed my eyes again and saw a stern

man. I told Carol that a man was coming forward and he seemed very stern.

"This man feels like your father," I told her.

"No!" she said loudly. "I don't want him to come into my reading! I met him when I was thirteen and he was an asshole! I don't want to hear from him!"

"I wish I could send him away, but he's coming forward so if I don't convey his message to you then I can't hear the rest of the reading," I replied.

She crossed her arms and was quiet again.

"He's saying he's sorry. He's holding a stick. I assume that means he was abusive?" I ventured to ask.

Carol nodded and started to cry again.

"But this can't be him because he never apologized for anything," she said.

I explained this process to Carol, "I want you to know that when spirits cross over, they have shown me that they go through a light and become a pure soul again. While making the transition to the other side, they have to do a life review. They have to look at the life they lived and they are either happy with that life or they are not. If they are not happy with how they lived their life, they try to help people here on earth heal in the areas where they caused pain. From what I have felt, they do this only to help you heal. Yes, they receive healing from it too, but they would help you even if it didn't benefit them in any way. He is appearing before me as a little kid and showing me that he wasn't always like this, and he mentions being abused as well. He is saying that he wasn't able to break the chain of abuse."

I continued, "He points to you and tells me that you were able to break the chain of abuse, and he is proud of you for that." He's also saying 'Principal,' are you a principal?"

"I am applying for that position right now," Carol stated.

"Please know he is aware of that," I shared with her. He says he's very proud of you and he's sorry he wasn't able to give you his love and support while he was here, but he's trying to do that now."

Carol later said she felt as if she'd gotten a mental massage from the reading. She also said she had gotten the position as a principal and thought her dad and great aunt had something to do with it because there were so many other suitable applicants.

EDWARD

Edward came in for a reading because his father had referred him to me. He was a tall motorcyclist who barely fit in my office chair. At first, I was startled by his rough attire, but I soon realized he was a gentle giant.

I held Edward's hand, closed my eyes, and set my intention, "God and Angels, please show me what you want me to know about Edward."

The image of a tree house appeared before me. It looked like a tree house for adults, not children.

I said, "This is the most interesting thing I have ever seen," I said. "Do you have a tree house on your property that adults use?"

"Dude, that's crazy," he said chuckling. "My friends call my house a tree house because I have a tree growing through the middle of the house. It comes up through the floor and out the ceiling in an atrium. It was there when I bought the house and I just liked the feeling of having it there so I never took it out."

"I'm seeing an older man, feels like a grandfather, with a cowboy hat on," I said. "He's cleaning hotel rooms, which doesn't make sense to me. Does any of this make sense to you?"

"My grandfather owned a hotel in Texas," Edward explained. "And he always wore a cowboy hat."

"Oh good, this is how he's coming through to me. He's showing me a cruise ship. Did you ever go on a cruise with him?" I asked.

"No, but I just got back from a cruise," Edward replied.

"Okay, good," I said. "Sometimes the

spirits show me things going on around you so you know they're nearby and are aware of what's going on."

I continued, "Now I hear change jingling in his pocket, and he's whistling."

"Yes," Edward confirmed, "that man was always whistling. He told me if I was ever in a bad mood, just start whistling and it would turn my day around. Now I whistle every day and it drives my friends nuts."

We both laughed. I find that laughing and crying are cathartic and makes the reading flow better. I don't know why, but they do.

I closed my eyes again and saw a

grandmother.

"There is an elderly woman showing me her shoes," I explained. "She is either looking for her shoes or something is wrong with them."

"Um, I don't know what that means," Edward responded.

Sometimes I feel like I'm playing charades with the spirits on the other side, trying to decipher what they're showing me.

"Was there something unusual about her feet?" I asked.

"Oh man!" Edward exclaimed. "Yeah, she

lost her leg because she was diabetic and only had one foot."

"Okay, that's it. That's why she's showing me her feet and making me feel like something was different about them." I nodded.

Then I heard the song "Puff the Magic Dragon." When I shared this with Edward, he looked stunned.

"My grandmother and I watched that movie over and over again when I was little," he shared. "It was my favorite movie."

Edward's eyes filled with tears. This was a precious memory and I was happy to be able to share it with him.

"She and your grandfather love you very much and are always around, watching over you," I said. "Now, your grandmother is pointing to your teeth and she's making me feel like you should get something looked at. She's showing me tobacco, but I feel like she is showing me chewing tobacco. Does this make sense to you?"

"Yeah," he said, hanging his head. "She never liked that I chewed it and wanted me to stop."

I replied, "Okay, I never hear bad things in my readings, but I do hear warnings, and she's screaming in my ear and telling me that you should stop. I also feel like it may be affecting your gums or your teeth and that you should get your teeth looked at right away."

"That makes sense. I haven't been to the dentist in about three years because I hate going, but I will go if she says I should," said Edward.

I continued, "The spirits are asking me to tell you the signs they use to show you that they're around you. Feathers are a sign, as well as coins, like the ones your grandfather kept loose in his pocket. I also keep hearing the song from that movie, *Puff the Magic Dragon*. If that song comes on the radio, know that it is a sign from your grandmother."

Edward started to laugh so hard his eyes watered.

"Ma'am, there is no way that song is going to come on the radio," he said. "The only place I listen to the radio is at work and I am a steelworker. We play hard rock or nothing at all."

"I understand what you're saying," I said, "but your grandmother is very stubborn and is making me feel like she will play that song for you."

"Okay," he said. "She was stubborn, that's for sure."

After the reading, Edward got up to leave. He gave me a huge hug goodbye, and because of his size, it reminded me of Hagrid hugging Harry Potter.

The next month I received a voicemail from Edward. He'd been working in the shop when, all of the sudden, *Puff the Magic Dragon* came on the radio. One of his coworkers tried to change the station, but Edward told him to leave it.

"I had to go to the restroom after the song was over because I was crying like a baby," he shared. "I still can't believe that song came on at my shop. Anyway, thank you for telling me about the signs. That's really cool."

JENNY & ERIN

Two sisters, Jenny and Erin, came to see me. They had been wanting to get a reading from someone and a friend of theirs had given them a flyer to one of my Angel classes. My classes give me the ability to talk about my gift and give readings to the attendees. These specific readings are "mini" readings. Jenny and Erin wanted something more in-depth.

I started their reading by closing my

eyes and saying, "God and Angels, please show me what you want me to know about Jenny and Erin."

The Angels showed me two little girls. They gave me the feeling that the girls grew up in foster care or someone else's home. I shared this image with Jenny and Erin.

Erin looked at Jenny and Jenny said, "Yes, that's true."

I continued, "I see a woman coming forward, but I can't understand what she's saying. Usually when this kind of energy comes through, it's because someone is regretful about their loved one's passing.

Maybe you didn't get there in time to say goodbye. Other times, I feel this way because they were responsible for how they passed away. Maybe they drank, or used drugs, or took their own life. I can't tell what was done, but the energy is very numbing for me."

Jenny grabbed Erin's hand.

I was then shown an image of a bottle of pills. When I told Jenny and Erin, they nodded and began to cry.

"I feel like you guys were very young when this happened, but Jenny, it's almost like you feel responsible for this, like you feel that you could have stopped her or something," I explained.

"Yes," Jenny said through tears, "And I also didn't get a chance to say goodbye to her. The last time we spoke I told her she was a horrible mom, and I feel like she took her life because of what I said."

I took a deep breath, closed my eyes, and prayed that God and the Angels would lift us with healing energy so that I could continue the reading.

"No, it wasn't your fault. This had nothing to do with you," I explained. "Your mother is showing me a roller coaster and saying when things were good with her, they were really good. But when they were bad, they were awful. This had nothing to do with anything you two did, and she wants you to know that. I feel as though you are living with this guilt, and she wants to help remove that. She's showing me her pills again and I'm getting the feeling that she was addicted to pain pills. I also don't feel like she meant to commit suicide. I feel like she took a double dose, not realizing how many she took."

"Did she suffer? Can you see that for us?" Jenny asked. "We were both playing at a neighbor's house when she died."

Both girls were still crying and holding hands. I could tell they were very close and

home, and when we pass away, that's where we return. So there never is a goodbye, only a 'see you later.'"

Both girls smiled and Erin said, "You mentioned in your class that the spirits of those who have passed away try to show us signs that they are around, but I don't see any signs and I can't feel her around me. Why is that? In one of our readings from a different medium, they said she was caught in-between."

"I share only what I have seen in readings and, as far as the spirits have shown me, we all go back home," I explained. "You can call it heaven, or the other side, whatever you feel comfortable with. I've never encountered anyone who was stuck and couldn't cross over. I have, however, had people who were still healing on the other side because of how they treated people while they were here and because of how they left. Let me assure you that your mom is home. As far as signs go, your loved ones are trying to get your attention any way they can. When we mourn or regret something about their passing, the energy is so heavy that I feel it is difficult to decipher what a sign is. Let me ask your mom what her signs for both of you are."

After a brief pause, I said "She shows me rainbows and says they are a sign of hope. She talks about the date of her birthday and/or the date of her passing. So, pay attention to receipts, license plates, and odometers in the car. And she shows me white butterflies."

"Really? We have so many of them in our backyard!" Jenny exclaimed.

"And I have a tattoo on my back of a butterfly, along with the date she passed away." Erin added.

"That's wonderful! See how she's coming through and showing me that," I smiled.

Then, a song entered my mind and I

started laughing because of the type of song it was. "Okay, now bear with me here because this seems kind of crazy," I said, "but did your mom like the song "Brick House'?"

"Yes," they said, laughing. I laughed along with them.

"I can see her dancing in the kitchen, and I hear laughter in the background."

"Yes, she would always do that and we would say 'Mom, knock it off,' but it made us laugh," the girls explained.

"I'm glad she's coming in so clearly. See how this works?" I asked. "When I first brought her forward, the energy was slow and heavy for me to read, but now that you have a better idea of what happened, the energy is higher."

They both agreed.

"Your mother wants me to tell you that she's aware of the pain she caused you," I said. "She's not excusing her behavior, but she's saying that addiction ran in the family. She's saying you girls learned from her how bad addictions can be and you both are breaking the chain by not going down the same path she did."

The girls smiled.

A week later, I received a text from Erin. She said she'd been looking for signs and she remembered me saying to look for numbers on receipts because her mother would use the date she passed away or her birthdate. Erin said that she always went to Starbucks before work and ordered the same items so the cost was always the same, but this time the price was different, $4.25.

"My mom passed away on April 25th," she said.

I told her that I thought it was wonderful that her mother was showing her signs like that in such an amazing way.

LAURA

Laura had been searching for mediums in her area and contacted me through my Yelp page. When she first called to set up an appointment, she was very cautious and asked a lot of questions about my credentials and how long I had been giving readings. Laura apologized for the lengthy inquiry, but I said I was glad she was doing her research. I love what I do, but I'm aware there are mediums out there who are not authentic, and for that reason I was glad she was being cautious.

"Is there something that would stand out about an unethical medium so I would know?" she asked. "Since I'm not aware of how this works, I'm not even sure I could spot someone who wasn't ethical."

I answered, "If a medium tells you that you've been cursed and that you need to visit him/her more times until the curse is broken, that's a sign that they're unethical. A medium should never tell how many times you need to see them, and I don't believe a person is ever 'cursed.' I believe we have challenges in life that can be difficult to get through, but that's how life is and we all have things to overcome. If a medium is reading you, but not giving you accurate information, then that's not right. And if a medium gives you advice that doesn't resonate with you, then follow your gut and don't listen to them."

Laura finally decided to make an appointment with me. She was a very classy lady who wore a dress with heels and carried a purse that seemed to match her shoes perfectly. I told Laura that I would now set my intention.

I took her hand, closed my eyes, and said, "God and Angels, please show me what I need to know about Laura." After a pause, I said, "I have a loved one stepping forward and he is showing me that he was in the Navy."

"No," she said, "I don't have any loved ones who have crossed over that were in the Navy."

I closed my eyes again and kept seeing the same man.

In my mind I said to him, "Show me something else because she isn't recognizing you."

He showed me a car accident. And I shared that with Laura.

"No," she answered. "I don't have a loved one who would fit that description."

I closed my eyes again and asked for another description so she would know the identity of the man who came forward. He showed me five pairs of the same pants and five identical blue short-sleeved shirts with a comb in the pocket.

I shared this image with Laura and she still said, "No."

I repeated all of the images together hoping they would help Laura recall who this was.

"Okay, he's a man who was in the Navy, and also in a car accident. This man wore the same clothes all the time and had a black comb in his pocket. Is this reminding you of anyone?" I asked.

"Well, yes," she said, "my late husband."

"Oh," I said, "do you remember me telling you that there is a loved one coming forward, that is what I meant, so this man is your late husband."

"Yes, those are all of the things that describe my late husband, except I didn't love him and you said 'loved one,'" Laura explained. "He was an alcoholic, and I fell out of love with him years before he passed away."

I could tell Laura was a good student, as

I had previously encouraged her to be skeptical of mediums. I came to find out, she was very literal so it took longer than usual for me to explain that if I got four out of five things right about a person who had crossed over, then that was confirmation that I was talking to the right person on the other side. Laura slowly began to understand.

Next, Laura asked about Ginger.

"I really miss her. Can you see anything about her?" she asked.

I closed my eyes and asked God and the Angels to show me anything regarding Ginger. I was shocked by what I saw because I could see a baby blanket and some toys buried with a body in what felt like someone's backyard. This was a first for me so I was extremely careful about sharing what I was seeing.

"Um, this is interesting," I said. "I'm seeing someone buried with their baby blanket and their baby toys."

"Yes, yes," she began to weep, "That was my Ginger, that's how we buried her."

"Okay, good," I said. "Then I know she's showing me this and just confirming that she is aware that you buried her that way."

"Is she in heaven?" Laura asked.

"Well," I explained, "Spirits that have crossed over have shared with me that they come from a loving place before they come here, and when they pass away, that's where they return. For me they've referred to that place as home, but for you it's heaven, and I believe it's one and the same."

"Good," said Laura, pulling out a white handkerchief from her purse.

I kept seeing the vision of Ginger being buried in the backyard.

"Laura, there was something else I was seeing," I said. "I felt like Ginger was showing me that she was buried in your backyard or close to where you live."

"Yes, that's right," she replied. "We've buried all our pets in our backyard because we loved them and wanted to keep them close."

"Oh, so Ginger was a cat?" I asked.

"Yes," she said, very seriously. I bit my lip, trying not to laugh.

I wasn't laughing at Laura. I also have pets that have become family members. I was laughing at myself because the entire time I was reading Laura, I thought they buried a baby in their backyard, and I was relieved to hear that Ginger was a cat.

DAVID

David was referred to me by his counselor, who thought I might be able to help him. I could tell that David wouldn't normally have gone to someone like me, unless it was because nothing else was working. I told David how I received my information and how long I'd been giving readings; I felt like explaining the process would put him at ease a bit.

I then took David's hand and set my

intention, "God and Angels, please show me what I need to know about David."

I could tell his heart was hurting, and I wanted to cry because I could feel his pain.

"I feel like you are heartbroken," I said.

"I guess you could say that," he replied.

"Did someone die before you were able to see them in the hospital?" I asked.

"No, but they died when I left the hospital room," he said, fidgeting in his chair.

"Was it your son?" I asked.

"Yep," David replied, trying to hold back his tears as he began to cry.

"I should have never left his hospital room, but I had to go to the bathroom and then I stopped to get some coffee and that's when he...."

David couldn't finish his sentence. He just shook his head as the tears rolled down his face.

I took a deep breath and closed my eyes. In my mind, I said to his son, "Sweetie, please show me something about your dad to help him heal."

The little voice said, "Tell him it's not his fault. He stayed with me the entire time."

I shared that message with David. Then I

told him that there have been so many times in my readings where people have passed away right when their family member left the room. I added that my mom did that right before my children and I got to the hospital, too, so I understood how he felt.

"It's almost like they love us so much they can't bear leaving us," I said. "So, the moment we leave, they jump to the other side. Once they have passed away, they are met with relatives on the other side. No one ever passes away alone. Those relatives comfort them and help them with their journey back home to the loving source.

They know that one day they will see us there so they are not as sad as we are when they leave. I do believe they miss our physical touch, but as I said, they know that this is not 'goodbye,' but 'see you later.'"

I continued, "In my readings I can see that those who have passed away are still around us and although their bodies have dissipated, their spirit is still alive, as is their love for us. It is with this love that they can send us signs that they are around us and watching over us."

David asked me if I could ask his son how he passed away. I told David that I couldn't see how his son passed away, which is one of my frustrations as a medium. I can't see everything, although for the sake of my clients, I wish I could so that I could give them more validation. Once I connect with their loved one on the other side, that person gives me the messages that they want to give.

"Your son is showing me swimming. Does this make sense to you?" I asked.

"Yes," David replied, "he was on a swim team."

"Okay, good," I said. "This is how it works: The spirits of loved ones who have passed away start off with small things that can then lead to something else. Your son is also showing me how much your family loves Disneyland. You guys are basically Disney fanatics, is that right?"

David chuckled a bit and that made me happy to see.

"That's very true," he answered. "We went to Disneyland all the time, probably more than we needed to. Is he showing you this?"

"Yes, once I connect with the spirits, they start to show me all kinds of things about them so you know their identity," I answered.

David nodded.

I closed my eyes again.

"Do you fly airplanes or have model airplanes?" I asked.

"Yes, I do," David said. "And my son and I would build them and fly them together."

"I am also seeing horses. Do you have horses?" I asked.

"No, but my mom does," David said. "He spent a week at her house every summer."

"Great, I'm glad he's confirming all of this for you," I shared. "Your son is making me feel like he had a great life with you, and it may have been cut short because of an illness, true?" David nodded.

"He's telling me that it was more time than most kids get with their fathers."

I continued, "Your son is also saying that you are the best dad in the world, and he had such a great life with you. You did so many things for him, and with him, that he doesn't want his last moments to define his entire life. He understands it's hard to do because you miss him so much, but please try, he says. He loves you very much, and it's important for you to know that. He doesn't want you to beat yourself up any more for leaving the hospital room."

I paused for a moment, "Your son is

making me laugh. He's making me feel that no matter what trouble he got into, it was hard to stay mad at him because of the 'look' he would give. The look of innocence- sweet eyes and a big smile. In other words, he was a good kid, but knew how to work you and was hard to say 'no' to."

"That's exactly it," David said, with a broad smile.

I continued, "So now that you know what his message is, he would like you to try to focus on the happy times, which consisted of ninety-five percent of his existence, rather than the five percent, which revolve around his passing. Does this make sense?"

"Yes, it does," David said. "I have to say that when my counselor first told me about you, I thought there is no way I am going to come and see this woman, but I was at the point where I knew I needed to try something. There is no way you could have known the things you told me, so I do believe you're talking to him. Can you tell him that I love him?"

"You just did," I answered. "He can hear you, and he knows that you've been talking to him, especially when you're driving. He says sometimes you cry in your truck because you don't want your wife to see that you've been crying, but she needs to see you cry and maybe you guys might even cry together because, in a way, you are the only ones who really know what you're going through and therefore, need to be each other's support system."

"Wow," David replied. "To be honest with you, that blows me away that you just said that. It's all true. Okay, so you're saying I can talk to him?"

"Yes, and you have been, and he hears you," I said. "Now, I was born with this gift so my ability to listen to the other side is a bit heightened, but we all have this capability. And even if you don't physically hear a response from him, just keep asking him to show that he is near you; he will show you. Since he mentioned his love for Disneyland, please know that he will use that symbol when he sends you a sign, letting you know that he's around."

"Okay," said David. "Thank you very much. I feel at peace now. I am still sad because I miss him, but there is peace in knowing his spirit is still alive, and like you said, he's just waiting for me on the other side, and I will see him again someday. I feel better knowing that."

Two months after the reading, David said

he was looking for signs from his son. He had been talking to him a lot, but was getting frustrated because he felt like nothing was happening, and he so desperately wanted to see a sign. One night, while he and his wife were watching television, the channel changed by itself; nobody was near the remote. The movie the television switched to was *Peter Pan*. David said that he and his wife knew this was a sign from their son, Andrew. Not only did the television change the channel on its own, but it landed on one of his son's favorite Disney movies.

CHAPTER 6
IN CLOSING

When I was younger, I remember knowing God and speaking to him every night. While lying in bed, I would clasp my hands together over my chest and pretend that I was filling my hands up with the love from my heart. Then, I would cup my hands together, making sure not to let any of the love seep out. I would then kiss my cupped hands and throw all my love up through the ceiling and into the sky.

I pictured God receiving this love and then sending it back down to me like a toy parachute. I would catch the parachute and place the love back in my heart. Laying my hands over my heart, I would smile, or cry, because I could feel the love as it entered my heart. I could feel God's love for me and knew that one day, with his support, I would help people by speaking and by writing books. It all seemed so real and felt so right.

As I grew older, I forgot about God and the loving source that God provided. Before acknowledging my gift as a medium, I felt scared, awkward, and alone in this world. After opening back up to my gift, I feel like I have found that assurance again. Now that I have accepted my purpose and reconnected to this loving source, I feel happy and comfortable in my own skin. It feels like I am home.

I hope my story has helped you realize that you are not alone. Though your loved ones have passed away, they are still very much around you, providing love and support from the other side. While on the other side, they experience a life review and once they have it, they want to help us in any way they can. They miss not being able to physically touch us, but they understand that we will all be together again one day.

In my readings, I have asked the spirits, who have passed away, where they are. They say we all come from a loving source and we come here to the earth's plane to share our gifts and our love with one another. When we pass away, we return to that loving source. When I ask them what they call this loving source, they say they call it "Home."

ABOUT THE AUTHOR

Julie Dart has been a certified medium since 2008. She received her Bachelor of Science from Cal Poly, San Luis Obispo. Julie has used her intuitive gift to give readings to radio listeners and to help the police and FBI with various cases. In addition, she is a teacher and author with a passion for writing children's books. Her books include: *The Night the Moon Was Hiding*, *Ellie Stands Up to the Bully*, and *Laila Saves the Day*. To schedule a reading or learn about upcoming books and events in your area, go to: www.dartpublishinghouse.com.

Made in the USA
Columbia, SC
16 July 2019